SONOMA

PHOTOGRAPHY BY ANDY KATZ WITH INTRODUCTION BY JAMES LAUBE

Published in 2010 by Andy Katz Photography
4982 West Soda Rock Lane
Healdsburg, California, 95448 USA
Tel. 707.433.9396
www.andykatzphotography.com

Library of Congress
Cataloging-in-Publication Data

ISBN 0-9649805-7-0

SONOMA
Photographs by Andy Katz
Introduction by James Laube

Printing: Mondadori, Verona, Italy

First Edition

10 9 8 7 6 5 4 3 2 1

Book Design: www.sodarockstudios.com

Photographs taken with the
SONY® α900
Lens: 24-70 f2.8, 16-35 f2.8,
70- 400 f2.8, 100 f2.8 macro

SONY
make.believe

Photograph Index

A special thank you to the people who helped make this book possible.

Jim Laube for his enthusiastic and passionate portrayal of Sonoma.

Honore Comfort of the Sonoma County Vintners,

Dan Wildermuth and Robert Larsen of Rodney Strong Vineyards and

Kayla Lindquist of Sony for their encouragement and support.

Ellen Riendeau of Soda Rock Studios for her photo editing and beautiful book design.

And I especially want to thank Tom Klein, proprietor of Rodney Strong Vineyards.

His love of Sonoma County, its vineyards and wines, is one big reason why

Sonoma is so extraordinary.

To the place I am fortunate enough to call my home, Sonoma.

Andy Katz

THE MAGIC OF SONOMA

The magic of Sonoma is impossible to miss–there is no place on Earth quite like it when it comes to sheer beauty, and few can rival it for fine-wine diversity and amazingly beautiful vineyards.

Sonoma boasts a spectacular, rock-studded coastline that embraces the magnificent Pacific Ocean, at times tranquil and mesmerizing, at other times wild and forbidding. Sonoma's marine-influenced climate dictates which grapes succeed. Thick summer fogs blanket the land mornings and nights and on moody wintry days. Vineyards thrive among the region's assorted soil types, its shifting topography and its different exposures, with the diversity of sites nurturing a variety of delicious wines.

Sonoma offers a little bit of everything when it comes to wine. We savor delicate, fragrant Rieslings and racy Sauvignon Blancs. We choose among rich, Burgundian-style Chardonnays and steely, flinty versions. Sonoma is home to an assortment of dazzling Pinot Noirs from Russian River and Sonoma Coast, bright and vivid with their zesty, raspberry flavors and sensual textures and earthier, layered renditions from Carneros hugging San Pablo Bay. We take pleasure in rustic Petite Sirahs and the peppery, wild berry intricacies of California's mystery grape Zinfandel. On display everywhere are infant vineyards budding their first clusters, and stumpy old vines planted a century ago.

In warmer inland sites, Cabernet Sauvignon, the great grape of Bordeaux, thrives, grown in fertile valley floors, on graceful sloping hillsides and atop rugged mountain peaks, giving us wines that showcase Cabernet's power and finesse, the iron fist in a velvet glove.

Sonoma is home to towering redwood trees, pristine rain-drenched forests, stark rolling hills, narrow valleys and crumbling mountains. The meandering Russian River cuts a path through the heart of the region, beginning its 100-mile journey north of the county line, where summer temperatures reach 100° F, and ending in Jenner, on the coast, where on the same summer day it might be a nippy 55°. The river winds through areas of extremes, some too cool and seemingly too remote for vineyards, yet most of Sonoma's terroir is perfect for some grape or another. The river reflects the diversity of the seasons. It can be a raging torment of muddy brown water in winter or a tranquil glimmering blue water host for a summer canoe ride.

I fell in love with Sonoma on my first visit many years ago, as a skinny 7-year-old on vacation with my family. My parents rented a small red-wood cabin on the river near Guerneville. It had a screened-in patio deck, a funky kitchen, bunk beds and a rickety wooden stairway that ended at a dock that floated on the river. From there my brothers and I frolicked in the water, rowing boats, catching fish, skipping stones, hiking through damp redwood forests and swinging from a thick tree rope and splashing into the water. It was as close to a bare-footed Huckleberry Finn summer adventure as a child could experience.

But even then the subtle, distinctive features of the Sonoma land-scape were evident and memorable to me, as were the ever-changing moods of the climate. We awakened to damp, foggy mornings, leaving us waiting anxiously for the fog to roll back. And by mid-morning, by nature's whimsical clock, the sun would appear and brighten the day. Then, after our full day of river fun, the fog would slowly and mysteriously begin to creep back inland over the tree-studded hills and cover the land like a fluffy down blanket.

It was a special, innocent time in my life, the start of an adventure so profound that it remains vivid today. Of course I had no idea that 20 years later I would fall in love with Sonoma once again, this time with a more specific purpose. First I experienced Sonoma's wine country as a curious guest, eager to taste the wines and then see where they came from and how they were made and by whom.

A few years later I came to know Sonoma in a more intimate way, with the start of a career writing about its magnificent vineyards and fascinating wines. The scenery in the Sonoma I love is mostly winding country roads, some smooth, some weathered, and almost all leading to or from a vineyard. The mountains are always there and so are the trees, giving dimension to every panorama, and the roads and vineyards bend according to the land's tilts and gaps. The scenery is interspersed with cows, horses, llamas and other farm animals. Dilapidated barns and homes are often not far from elaborate country mansions.

The portrait of Sonoma that Andy Katz provides us in this amazing essay of photographs is of its vineyards. He knows the region better than most, being a resident of Healdsburg and living among the vines. Here the face of Sonoma is the vineyard, framed and defined by its picturesque, pastoral countryside. The vineyards come in many shapes and sizes, from the tiniest of 1- or 2-acre plots on steep, isolated hilltops to vast vineyards draped over rolling hills and stretching for miles. Katz takes us places few outsiders know exist and captures their eloquent beauty, allowing us to pause and contemplate the intricacies of vineyards planted amidst stunning natural surroundings.

Katz shows us the life and colors of the seasons, from the barren, icy stillness of winter, to the tender push of the young vines in the spring when they awaken from their rest and begin to blossom, to the heart of the growing season, as the grape clusters take shape, color and ripen. At times Katz's photos are so dreamy as to blur the difference between still-life photography and an impressionist's painting. His eye allows us–perhaps even forces us–to study the detail, the lighting, the proportional dimensions of vineyards and how they communicate rhythm and texture in harmony with the land.

Today nearly 200 wineries call Sonoma home and nearly 50,000 acres are planted in vines for the sole purpose of making wine. Take time to pour yourself a glass of Sonoma's finest and absorb the passion of Sonoma that Andy Katz so brilliantly captures for us, a visual masterpiece that words can only attempt to describe.

- James Laube, Senior Editor *Wine Spectator*

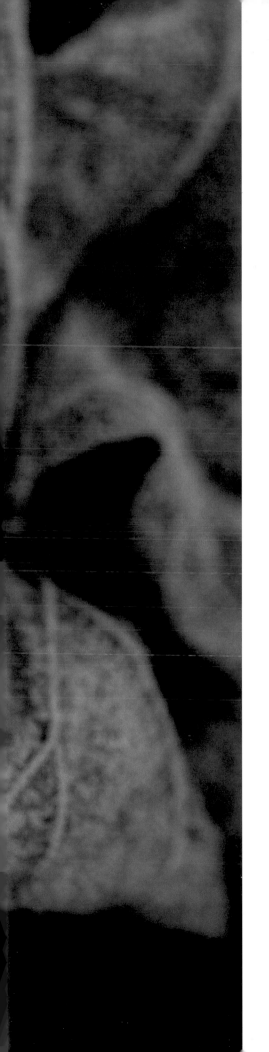